_____

To

_____

From

_____

Date

For Katy and Brinck, and children
of all ages everywhere . . .

My Friend Jesus

The Gospel for Kids

by Kathryn Slattery

illustrated by Alida Massari

Tommy NELSON®

A Division of Thomas Nelson Publishers

NASHVILLE DALLAS MEXICO CITY RIO DE JANEIRO

Published in Nashville, Tennessee, by Tommy Nelson. Tommy Nelson is a registered trademark of Thomas Nelson, Inc.

Published in association with the literary agency of Mark Sweeney and Associates, Bonita Springs, Florida 34135

Scripture quotations are taken from the Holy Bible, New International Version®, NIV®. Copyright © 1973, 1978, 1984, 2011 by Biblica, Inc™. Used by permission of Zondervan. All rights reserved worldwide. www.zondervan.com

Thomas Nelson, Inc., titles may be purchased in bulk for educational, business, fund-raising, or sales promotional use. For information, please e-mail SpecialMarkets@ThomasNelson.com.

Library of Congress Cataloging-in-Publication Data
Slattery, Kathryn.
  [Gospel for kids]
  My Friend Jesus / by Kathryn Slattery.
      pages cm
  "Originally published as The Gospel for Kids."
  ISBN 978-1-4003-2267-1
  1. Jesus Christ--Juvenile literature. 2. Bible stories, English--N.T.
Gospels. I. Title.
  BT302.S553 2013
  232--dc23
                              2013013942

Printed in China

13 14 15 16 17 TIMS 6 5 4 3 2 1

ALL NEW MATERIAL
Filling: Polyurethane Foam
REG. No. PA-14954 (CN), MA-3031 (CN)
Made in China

TSSA Reg. No 07T-00912512

A Note to Grown-Ups

Dear Friend,

If you are reading this, I suspect there is a very special child in your life—a child you love beyond measure, a child for whom you pray every day. And when you pray, I imagine that at the very top of your list of hopes and dreams for this precious child is *faith*. Faith in a loving, personal God. Faith that doesn't disappoint. Faith that is unchanging. Faith that lasts forever. I'm talking about *real* faith—the kind of faith that serves as a powerful source of guidance, hope, and protection in a world that can be filled with distractions, dangers, obstacles, and challenges. The Bible teaches that there is but one sure way to access this uniquely real, loving, personal, powerful, eternal faith—and that is through a relationship with Jesus Christ.

As the mother of two children, I understand that growing up isn't easy. Today more than ever, children need to be informed and reassured that *God is real*, that *He personally loves them*, and that *He has a unique purpose for each of their lives.*

I was nineteen years old—a bewildered and unformed college student, far away from home—before I ever heard the Christian gospel presented in a clear, easy-to-grasp, meaningful way. The word *gospel* literally means "good news." To this day, the moment I first heard the gospel and asked Jesus Christ into my heart remains the single most important, life-transforming, personally helpful event in my life.

Too bad, I've often thought, *so many years passed before I heard the gospel and believed.* Even as a small child—*especially as a child*—might I not have benefited from the priceless gift of a personal relationship with Jesus?

I wrote this gospel for children in direct response to questions about God and Jesus posed by my young daughter and son. Because it is for children, it is written in clear, easy-to-understand language for youngsters of all ages and denominations. And because it is for children, I emphasize the unique nature of Jesus as the ultimate friend. It is this, after all, that every person at every age yearns for . . .

A real friend.

A friend who is faithful. A friend who is all-forgiving. A friend you can trust. A friend whose presence makes you feel deep-down good inside. A friend who will laugh with you and cry with you. A friend you can call out to anytime, anywhere, and know that He will be there . . .

This is the friend I've come to know and love in Jesus Christ. This is the friend Jesus whom I hope my children and grandchildren and—through this book—children of all ages everywhere will come to know intimately and love as well.

Kitty Slattery

www.KathrynSlattery.com
Facebook: Kathryn "Kitty" Slattery

Greater love has no one than this:

to lay down one's life for one's friends. . . .

I have called you friends.

—John 15:13, 15

Long, long ago . . . ever so many years
after the creation of the world and
two thousand years before TV . . . a
baby boy was born in the tiny town of
Bethlehem, in the tiny country of Israel.

We know this is true.

It is not a myth, or legend, or fairy tale.

It is an honest-to-goodness historical fact.

But because it happened so many years
ago, long before there were things like
computers and the Internet, we don't
know for sure the exact day this baby
boy was born. Or the exact address.

We do know that He was born in a
stable, which is like a small barn.

He was born in a stable because
hospitals hadn't been invented yet and
because there was no room at any of
Bethlehem's inns for the baby's family,
who was visiting from out of town.

The baby's mother was named Mary. Her husband was a man named Joseph. But many months earlier, before Mary even knew she was going to have a baby, a beautiful angel named Gabriel visited her to share this great mystery:

"You are going to have a son," Gabriel announced to the astonished Mary. "And His true Father will be God in heaven."

As Gabriel instructed, Mary named her baby boy Jesus, which means *Savior*, or "One who saves the people."

And to this day, Jesus remains *the most important person who ever lived* in the history of our world.

Why is Jesus so important?

Because of who He is and because of the extraordinary things He said and did during His time here on earth.

What are some of the things Jesus said and did?

Well, for starters, Jesus said He was God's very own Son—and everyone knows how important God is!

Jesus was so close to God that when He prayed, or talked to God, He used the word *Abba*, which in Jesus' native Aramaic language means "Daddy" or "Papa."

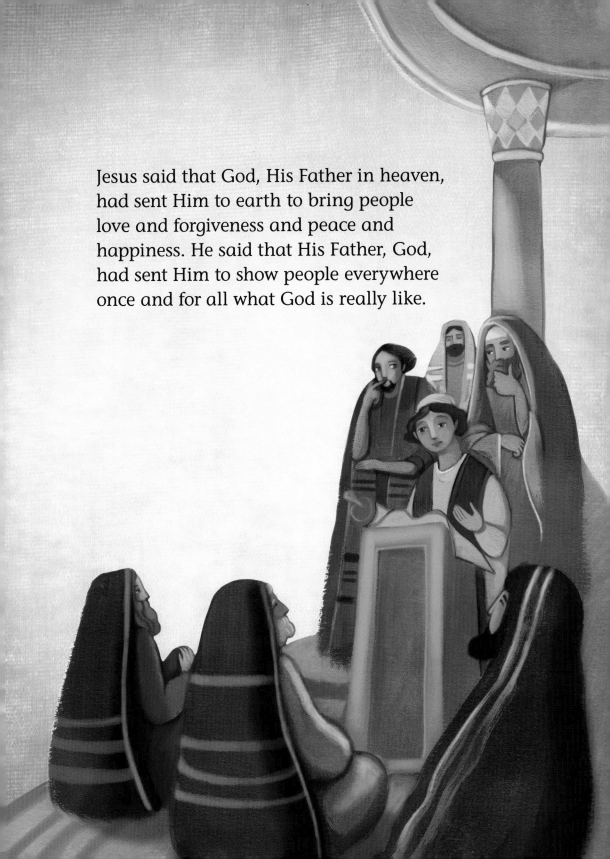

Jesus said that God, His Father in heaven, had sent Him to earth to bring people love and forgiveness and peace and happiness. He said that His Father, God, had sent Him to show people everywhere once and for all what God is really like.

When Jesus was born, it was as though God Himself put on skin and came crashing into human history!

Until Jesus was born, you see, no one had ever really seen God.

No one was sure what God was really like.

Was God friendly? Or was He grouchy? Was God happy? Or was He gloomy? Did God cry? Did God laugh? Did God even think or care much about His people at all? Or was He

too busy doing important things, like keeping the stars up in the sky and the planets from bumping into each other?

Jesus said that God cares *a lot* about each and every one of us—and that includes you and me.

"Listen to what I say, and watch what I do. I will show you what My Father, God, is like and how much He cares about you," Jesus said.

To show people what God is like, Jesus did a lot of loving, kindhearted things, like make sick people well, and lame people walk, and blind people see, and deaf people hear. Once He even brought a dead man named Lazarus back to life!

When people were sad, Jesus cried with them. When people were happy, He laughed with them. Jesus was a truly excellent friend.

Jesus did all these things to show how much God loves and cares for us and so that people everywhere—and that includes you and me—would believe that He really and truly is God's Son and so we would believe in God too.

There is another very
important thing about
Jesus. *He loved children.*

Although Jesus never got
married and had children
of His own, He deeply loved
all the boys and girls He met. And
the children loved Him back.

Grown-ups, Jesus said, could learn a lot
from children.

Children, He explained, are natural-born
experts when it comes to believing in God.

"Let all the children come to Me and believe
in Me and in My Father, God," Jesus said.
"And as for you grown-ups, you try to be
a little more like children this way as well.
Understand?"

Many of the grown-ups understood what
Jesus was trying to teach them, and they
loved Him.

But others didn't.

And when Jesus was still a young man, just thirty-three years old, He was killed—put to death on a wooden cross—by fearful, unhappy people who didn't understand the things He said and did. Jesus was killed by people who just couldn't find it in their hearts to believe Him. Jesus was killed by people who had forgotten how to be like children in their hearts.

Now, since Jesus was God's Son, He could have stopped these people from killing Him. But He didn't. By choosing to give up His life, He took upon Himself the punishment for all the bad things people do and think.

Jesus died to save everyone on earth who would believe in Him. That's why He is called our Savior.

People were so sad on the day Jesus died!

His mother, father, family, and friends—all of them missed Him terribly. They cried and cried.

If only Jesus could somehow come back and be with us, they thought.

But that was impossible. Never again would they hear the sound of Jesus' laughter, listen to His stories, or feel His big, strong hugs.

They took His broken, lifeless body and laid it gently in a tomb, which was like a small, dark room with a dirt floor, carved into the side of a grassy hill. The strongest men rolled a big rock over the opening to the tomb, and then—their hearts nearly breaking with sorrow—they all walked away.

Early in the morning, three days after Jesus died, Jesus' friend—a woman named Mary Magdalene—set off to visit the tomb where Jesus' body had been laid. But when she arrived, the big stone that had covered the opening to the tomb had been rolled away. Even stranger, the tomb was empty. Where had the body of her beloved Jesus gone?

Soon after that, Mary made the most wonderful, important, extraordinary discovery . . .

Jesus was alive!

The tomb was empty because Jesus—in the most mysterious, awesome, miraculous way—was no longer dead *but had come back to life!*

How happy everyone was to see and be with Jesus again!

Once again, Jesus talked and laughed with His mother, family, and friends. He even had a picnic on the beach with some of His best friends. Once again, they all gathered around Him and listened to His stories.

Jesus said that soon He would be going back to heaven to live with His Father, God. But before He left, He had some very good news.

Everyone leaned forward and listened carefully.

"The good news," Jesus said, "is that because I have come back to life, you too can live forever with Me and My Father in heaven. God loves you so much that He wants this for you. He wants you to believe in Him and Me. He wants to forgive you when you make mistakes. He wants you to live with Him forever."

Jesus explained to His family and friends that because they loved and believed Him, after their lives on earth ended, they would find themselves alive in heaven with God and Him.

It will be such a happy time! Like a big birthday party.

This is because everyone in heaven is happy and healthy. Everyone in heaven has new bodies that live forever, and there is no more sadness or crying or pain.

"In heaven," Jesus said, "God will wipe away every tear from every eye."

Jesus told His family and friends one last thing before He returned to heaven to live with God. Jesus told them that although He could no longer stay with them in person, God had arranged a special way that He could be with them in their hearts.

"I will send you My Holy Spirit," Jesus said. "He will live in your hearts and teach you, guide you, and comfort you— just the way I've been able to do while I've been with you here on earth."

True to His promise, that is exactly what Jesus did.

Even today, right now, Jesus can be alive in our hearts through His Holy Spirit.

Even today, it is possible to listen to His voice . . . hear His laughter . . . even feel His hugs.

Do you know what Jesus wants right now, more than anything?

Jesus wants to live in your heart.

More than anything, Jesus wants to be your friend.

The kind of friend who will help you know right from wrong. The kind of friend who will forgive you when you make mistakes and love you no matter what. The kind of friend who is fun to be with and will make you feel deep-down good inside.

Jesus wants to be the kind of friend you can talk to when you're sad, when you're happy, when you're lonely, when you're scared—anytime at all!

Yes, more than anything, Jesus wants to be your Savior and friend—the best friend you ever had.

If you're not sure that Jesus is living in your heart, would you like to ask Him to be your friend?

It's easy.

All you have to do is call His name and let Him know. Like this:

Hi, Jesus! I just want to let You know that I believe in You and in Your Father, God. Thank You for forgiving me when I make mistakes and for loving me the way You do. Please come into my heart now and live in me and be my friend.

I love You, Jesus. And I'm really excited about being Your friend too.

Once you've prayed this prayer (for that's all prayer really is—talking to Jesus!), you will begin a new adventure in your life unlike any other. Wherever you go, whatever you do, Jesus will be with you, living in your heart, helping and loving you.

Whenever you want Him, just call His name. Say, "Hi, Jesus!" and He will be with you—listening, caring, being the *best friend* you ever had.

Now that you've reached the end of this story, you are about to begin a brand-new story.

A real, true-life story.

A story that begins here and now.

In your heart.

It is the story of your new life and special friendship with Jesus.

Have fun!